# Needleturn Appliqué
## The basics & beyond

## by Angela Lawrence

Landauer Publishing, LLC

# Needleturn Appliqué
## The basics & beyond
### by Angela Lawrence

Copyright© 2012 by Landauer Publishing, LLC
Project designs copyright© 2012 by Angela Lawrence

This book was designed, produced,
and published by Landauer Publishing, LLC
3100 101st Street, Urbandale, Iowa 50322
www.landauercorp.com   800/557-2144   515/287-2144

President/Publisher: Jeramy Lanigan Landauer
Vice President of Sales & Administration: Kitty Jacobson
Editor: Jeri Simon
Art Director: Laurel Albright
Photographer: Sue Voegtlin

ISBN 13: 978-1-935726-17-3
ISBN 10: 1-935726-17-x

This book is printed on acid-free paper.

Printed in China by C&C Offset Printing Co.,Ltd.

10 9 8 7 6 5 4 3 2 1

Needleturn Appliqué, The basics & beyond
Library of Congress Control Number: 20011943407

# Introduction

Appliqué is the process of layering one fabric onto a larger fabric surface. Today there are a variety of different ways to appliqué by hand or machine. The needleturn appliqué method is considered the traditional technique. This method utilizes the needle as your main tool for turning under seam allowances and securing the appliqué shapes to the background fabric. It requires small, consistent hand-stitches that seem to disappear.

For centuries quilters have created appliqué quilts without the elaborate resources we enjoy today. They did not have the fabrics and notions that are now available, and yet they created beautiful, heirloom appliqué quilts that are still cherished. Surely they must have enjoyed the needleturn appliqué handwork. It is my hope that this book will instill that "love of handwork" in you.

After years of teaching needleturn appliqué, I have brought the basic techniques that I teach and endorse in my classes together into a book. Through the inclusion of a thorough supply list, informative preparation instructions, as well as illustrations of the actual needleturn appliqué stitch, you have all the resources you need to become proficient in needleturn appliqué. A chapter devoted to color and fabric selection has also been included to enhance your quilting experience. The basic color principles outlined will provide a starting point for success in the fabric selection process. This book includes nine fun and unique appliqué projects in a variety of color ways, so you will have multiple opportunities to perfect your needleturn skills.

*Angela*

# where to find it

# getting started—basics & beyond

You will find everything you need to know to begin your needleturn appliqué journey on the following pages. I have been teaching students this needleturn appliqué technique for many years with great success. Each skill is shown in clear, close-up photography and detailed instructions with useful tips scattered throughout. The project section offers some of my favorite unique designs with full-size patterns. Watch for quilts throughout the book labeled Angela's Inspirations, these are perfect examples of going beyond a basic project while still using the myriad of techniques you have learned.

*Angela*

**Equipment & Supplies** offers important information on selecting tools and supplies for needleturn appliqué. My favorites are highlighted, but it is important to experiment with a variety of products to find what works for you.

**Color and Fabric Selection** will show you the importance of six key color elements. Hue, value, intensity, scale, temperature, and texture should always be taken into consideration when selecting fabrics for your project.
You may be surprised to learn that choosing a color scheme before fabric shopping will make your trip to the quilt shop less overwhelming.

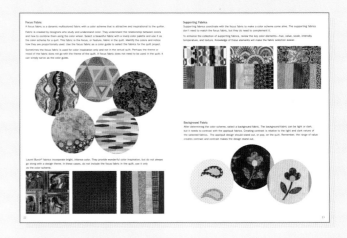

**Appliqué Preparations** offers alternate methods for preparing the appliqué shapes and transferring the designs. Practice each of the methods to determine which you prefer. Easy-to-follow directions and photographs will guide you through each technique.

You will also learn why it is important to number your pattern and each appliqué shape.

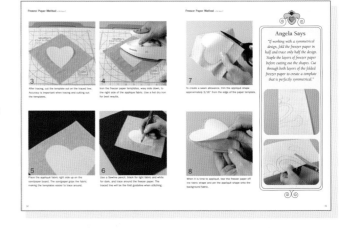

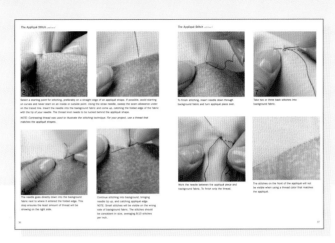

**Stitching the Appliqué** demonstrates how to begin and end the appliqué stitch. Close-up photography illustrates bringing the needle up through the fold of the appliqué shape and taking it back down into the background fabric. Contrasting thread was used to highlight the stitches and make the process easier to follow.

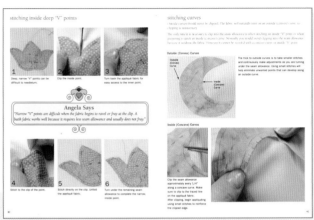

**Points and Curves** often appear daunting to needleturn appliquérs. Learn the tricks to stitching crisp inside and outside points, as well as deep "V"s. You will quickly master the technique of needleturning smooth convex and concave curves by following the clear step-by-step instructions and photography in this chapter.

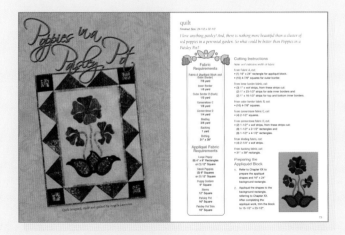

**Projects with full-size patterns** are included to encourage you to take the skills you have just learned and create something beautiful. Projects range from table runners to wall hangings to small quilts with color options added for extra inspiration. The full-size patterns make transferring the designs quick and easy.

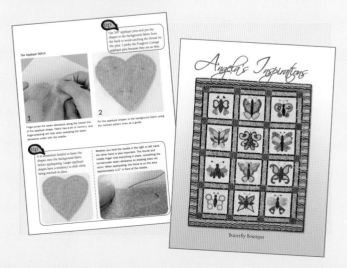

**Tips and Inspiration** are scattered throughout each technique. The tips offer helpful suggestions to make the needleturn process easier. The tips labeled "Angela Says" come from personal experience and years of teaching and sharing ideas with my students. Angela's Inspirations will spur you to go beyond a simple one-block quilt and create a multiblock masterpiece with the needleturn appliqué skills you have acquired.

# equipment & supplies

The following tools are my personal, tried-and-true favorites for needleturn appliqué. After many years of appliquéing and teaching, I have found these to be the most effective for the needleturn appliqué process. Experiment with these and other tools to determine what works best for you in mastering the needleturn appliqué technique.

# needle & thread

The needle is the most important tool to the needleturn appliqué quilter. Experiment with the large variety of needles available to determine which needle works best for you. A fine-quality thread in a color that matches the appliqué fabric is also necessary for needleturn appliqué. Have a large assortment of thread in an array of colors on hand.

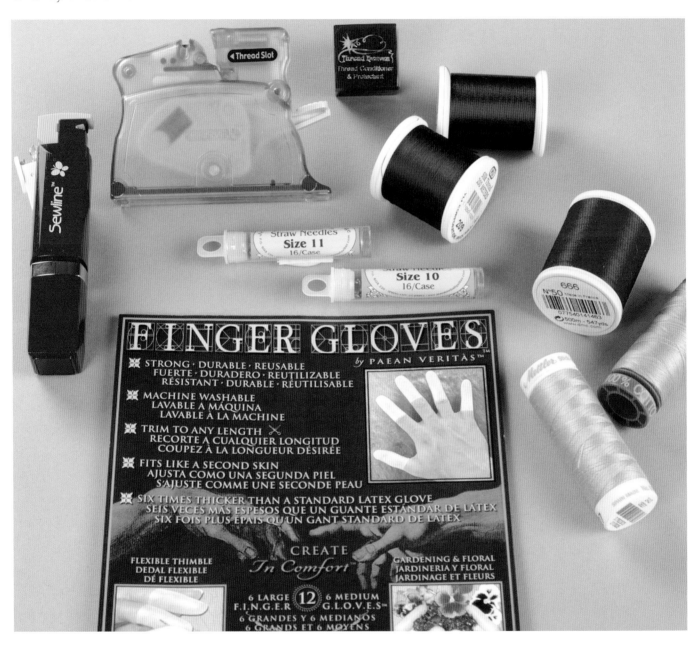

## Favorites

**needles and threads**

- Jeana Kimball Straw Needles
- YLI Silk Thread
- Kimono™ Silk Thread

- Mettler Metrosene Silk-Finish Cotton Thread 60-weight
- Aurifil™ Mako Cotton Thread 50-weight
- DMC® Cotton Thread 50-weight

### Straw Needles

The straw needle has a long, thin shank that glides easily through any fabric. Use size 10 or 11 straw needles when appliquéing. Size 10 straw needles work well with cotton fabrics. Size 11 straw needles have a thinner shank and work especially well with batik fabrics, which have a higher fiber count when compared to other cotton fabrics.

### Silk Thread

Silk 100-weight thread is a wonderful choice for needleturn appliqué. It is very fine and has a reflective quality that easily blends with cotton fabrics. This fine-weight thread buries itself between the cotton fibers and appears to be nearly invisible.

### Cotton Thread

When appliquéing with cotton thread, it is important to use a fine-weight thread. Depending on the brand, the weight of the thread is usually a two-ply 50- to 60-weight thread. The higher the thread number, the finer the thread weight.

My favorite cotton thread for appliqué is DMC® Cotton Thread 50-weight. It is a thin, durable appliqué thread that feels almost as fine as silk and comes in a large assortment of colors.

### Finger Gloves™

The Finger Gloves™ can be used in place of a thimble to protect your middle finger from the needle. They are a lightweight latex product that protects your finger while stitching without feeling heavy or bulky.

### Needle Threader

A needle threader is extremely helpful when trying to thread the small eye of a needle. My favorites are the Clover Needle Threader and the Sewline™ Needle Threader.

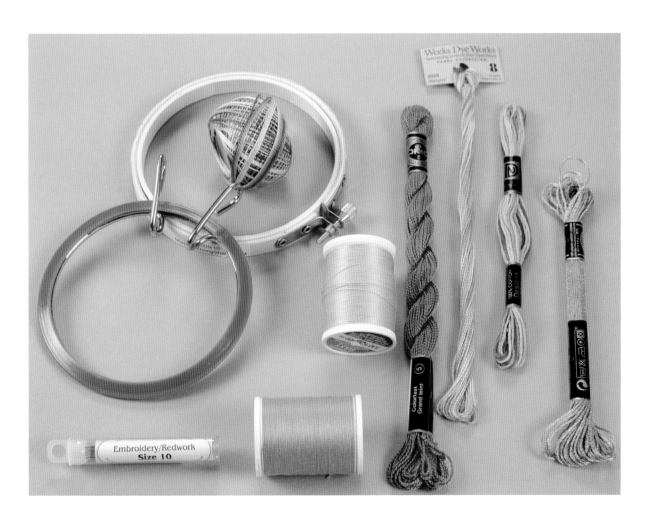

# scissors

There is a huge assortment of scissors available to quilters. The following scissors work well for the needleturn process.

### Karen K. Buckley Serrated Large Scissors

This scissors is great for cutting out appliqué fabric shapes. The fine serrated edge helps prevent the raw edge of fabric from fraying. Because of the large handles, it is comfortable to work with when cutting.

### Gingher 4" Large Handle Embroidery Scissors

This scissors features a very fine point which is necessary for clipping inside points and concave curves.

## appliqué pins

Appliqué pins secure the appliqué shapes in place while stitching. A 3/4"-long appliqué pin is less likely to catch the thread while stitching. Also, appliqué pins with rounded edges will prevent the thread from catching on the pinhead.

## Favorites

**appliqué pins**
- Foxglove Cottage 3/4" Appliqué Pins
- Clover Appliqué Pins

### Angela Says
*"Do not use your fabric scissors for cutting template plastic or freezer paper. This will dull the blades. Use separate scissors or fabric and paper."*

# marking tools

Before choosing a marking tool, know where you are going to use it. Some marking tools work better than others at certain tasks.

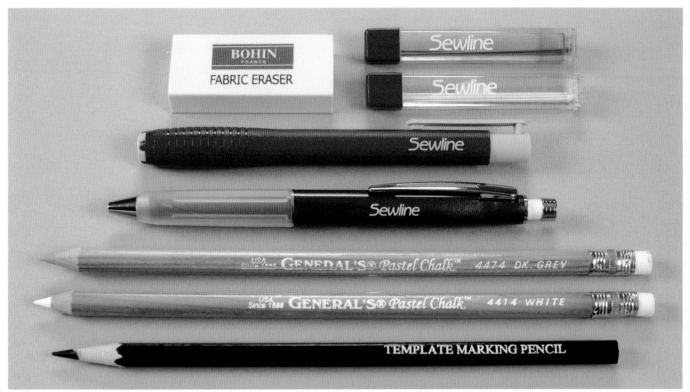

### Template Marking Pencil

This pencil is designed for tracing designs on the surface of template plastic.

### General's® Pastel Chalk Pencil
### (Dark Gray or White)

These chalk pencils work great when tracing the appliqué design onto the background fabric. The chalk markings can easily be removed from the fabric.

### Sewline™ Pencil (Gray and White)

This pencil has a very fine point and is used to trace the appliqué template shapes onto the appliqué fabrics.

### Fabric Eraser

Keep a fabric eraser on hand to take care of any tracing mistakes.

### Sandpaper Board

A sheet of sandpaper or a sandpaper board can be used to grip the appliqué fabric while tracing the appliqué shapes. A very fine-weight sandpaper is recommended.

tip

Avoid any chalk pencil with colored dye. The dye makes the tracings difficult to remove from fabric.

Always test a marking pencil before using it on your fabric. Make sure the marking can be removed from the fabric.

# template materials

Creating accurate templates is important in the needleturn appliqué technique. The curves need to be smooth and the points sharp. Keep this in mind when choosing your template material.

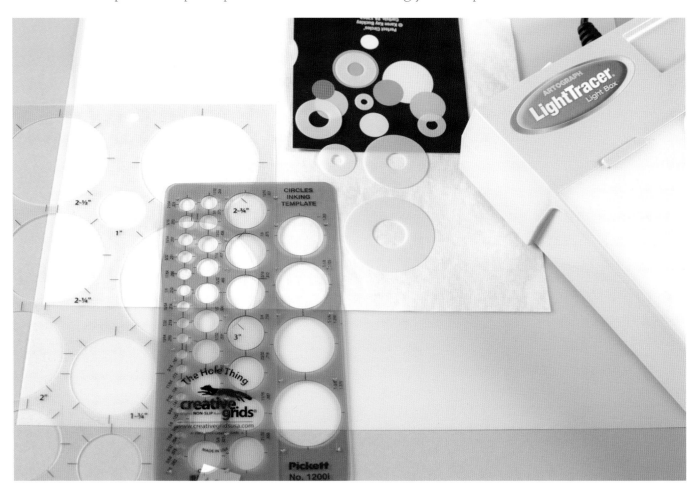

### Template Plastic

Template plastic is a good choice when creating templates that will be used repeatedly. If you are tracing an appliqué shape multiple times, the plastic will not lose its shape. The plastic sheets are transparent for ease in tracing.

### Freezer Paper

Freezer paper is a quick, easy, inexpensive way to create appliqué templates. Freezer paper is available on the roll at your local grocery store. It is also available in 8-1/2" x 11" sheets that can be run through the printer, eliminating the need for hand tracing.

### Nice, but not required

**Circle Templates** by Creative Grids® and **Perfect Circles®** by Karen Kay Buckley are two products that allow you to create accurate circles in a variety of sizes.

### Light Box

When tracing the appliqué design on the background fabric it is important to have a light source. A light box can be used to aid in the process of seeing and tracing a design through the background fabric.

### Nice, but not required

The proper amount of lighting is very important. There is a portable tabletop **Ott-Lite®** that is great for quilt retreats, classes or home. The Ott-Lite® is also available as a floor lamp.

### Overlay Material

Pattern Ease is a lightweight, transparent interfacing material that works great for tracing the appliqué pattern.

Fandango features layered appliqués, reverse appliqué, circles and bias stems.

# color and fabric selection

The right choice of fabric and color can turn your quilt from 'nice' to 'wow'. There are six key color elements to consider when selecting fabric. These elements will be referred to continually throughout this chapter.

# key color elements

When discussing guidelines for selecting fabrics, there are six key color elements. These elements should be kept in mind during the fabric selection process.

## hue

Hue is another word for color. The colors or hues selected for a quilt are important because they set the mood. For example, blue is calm and restful, red is high energy, and yellow says sunshine and cheer. Color is very personal and the emotion it releases varies with each individual. A person may decide they dislike a quilt simply because of the color scheme without any regard for the pattern or techniques used in it. The most important point to emphasize is that the person creating the quilt should feel confident with the fabrics that have been chosen.

## value

Value refers to the lightness and darkness of a color. Add white (tint) to a color to lighten its value. For example, red becomes pink when white is added. Add black (shade) to a color to darken its value. For example, red becomes maroon or burgundy when black is added. Using a variety of light and dark colors creates depth and dimension and enhances the quilt design. The color scheme is important for setting the stage of a quilt, but it is the range of color value that produces contrast and makes the pattern come alive.

 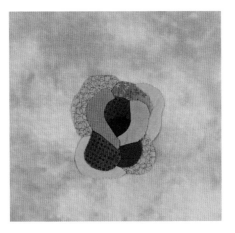 

The traditional quilt pattern, Tumbling Block, reinforces the color value concept. It is the light and dark color values that produce the dimensional effect of this quilt pattern.

Value is important when creating an intricate appliqué design. A budding red rose requires many fabrics in various color values to define its petals.

## intensity

Intensity refers to the brilliance of a color. High-intensity colors are pure, bright, vivid and saturated. Low-intensity colors are toned down and grayed. They create less contrast but blend together well. A succesful appliqué quilt will include high and low color intensity. Use high-intensity colors as an accent to draw attention to the important areas of your appliqué design.

High Color Intensity      Low Color Intensity

## scale

Scale refers to the size of the printed fabric motif or design. Fabric can be divided into three categories: large-scale, medium-scale and small-scale prints. The scale of the fabric should be taken into consideration when determining where to place the fabric in a quilt.

Small-scale prints work great for small appliqué pieces, while large-scale prints are often used as a border.

**tip**

Make a "window" out of cardboard in the shape of your appliqué piece to aid in selecting fabric.

## temperature

Temperature refers to the illusion of warmth and coolness a color portrays. Yellow, red and orange evoke warmth, as in a glowing fire. Blues and greens are cool and less energetic, as in water and mossy grass. Warm colors pop out in a quilt design, while the cool colors recede into the background.

Nature is the perfect example. Picture a beautiful flower garden with red, yellow and orange flowers set against a blue sky and green grass. The flowers draw the viewer's attention first, while the background colors recede. The same will happen in your appliqué quilt.

Warm Colors

Cool Colors

## texture

The element of texture is divided into two categories: tactile and visual.

Tactile texture refers to the texture you can feel and touch. An example of tactile texture can be found in the traditional crazy quilts and today's art quilts. Many different textured fabrics such as silk, velvet and satin are included in these quilts. Yarns, beads and buttons provide another layer of texture.

Traditional Crazy Quilt

Visual texture involves the illusion of texture seen by the eye. When creating an appliqué quilt, the visual texture is generally more important than the tactile texture. By including an assortment of printed fabrics as well as a variety of colorful, interacting appliqué shapes, you will achieve texture in the appliqué design.

Contemporary Art Quilt

Now that you are aware of the key color elements, it is time to apply this knowledge to your appliqué projects. After choosing initial fabrics for a project, lay them out and determine if the six key color elements are represented in your selection. You can now feel confident in your choice of fabric. Use the six key color element checklist whenever you begin a new project.

Visual Texture

# inspiration for the color scheme

The first step in making an appliqué quilt is to have a pattern or design concept in mind. Once that has been determined, you can begin to select your fabrics. With the large array of fabrics available, it is easy to become overwhelmed, so it is a good idea to establish a color scheme before fabric shopping.

Look at the world around you for inspiration. Color schemes can be found in natural outdoor settings, such as a summer flower garden or autumn trees. Nature provides amazing color inspiration—just look at a sunset.

Color inspiration can also be found in antique vases, oil paintings, upholstery fabrics, or a tapestry.

## Angela Says

*"If you are still having trouble selecting a color scheme, visit your local quilt shop. Quilt shops are filled with fabrics that can be used as the focus for a color scheme."*

## Focus Fabric

A focus fabric is a dynamic multicolored fabric with a color scheme that is attractive and inspirational to the quilter.

Fabric is created by designers who study and understand color. They understand the relationship between colors and how to combine them using the color wheel. Select a beautiful fabric with a lovely color palette and use it as the color scheme for a quilt. This fabric is the focus, or feature, fabric in the quilt. Identify the colors and notice how they are proportionally used. Use the focus fabric as a color guide to select the fabrics for the quilt project.

Sometimes the focus fabric is used for color inspiration only and not in the actual quilt. Perhaps the theme or mood of the fabric does not go with the theme of the quilt. A focus fabric does not need to be used in the quilt; it can simply serve as the color guide.

Laurel Burch® fabrics incorporate bright, intense color. They provide wonderful color inspiration, but do not always go along with a design theme. In these cases, do not include the focus fabric in the quilt, use it only as the color scheme.

## Supporting Fabrics

Supporting fabrics coordinate with the focus fabric to make a color scheme come alive. The supporting fabrics don't need to match the focus fabric, but they do need to complement it.

To enhance the collection of supporting fabrics, review the key color elements—hue, value, scale, intensity, temperature and texture. Knowledge of these elements will make the fabric selection easier.

## Background Fabric

After determining the color scheme, select a background fabric. The background fabric can be light or dark, but it needs to contrast with the appliqué fabrics. Creating contrast is relative to the light and dark values of the selected fabrics. The appliqué design should stand out, or pop, on the quilt. Remember, the range of value creates contrast and contrast makes the design stand out.

Stems blend into background fabric in this example.

Stems pop on background fabric in this example.

## Purchasing and Organizing Fabric

As you become more experienced you will discover some fabrics are better suited than others for needleturn appliqué. Look for tightly woven fabrics that have a thin feel. Avoid loose weave or bulky fabrics. A loosely woven fabric has a tendency to ravel while a tightly woven fabric is easier to needleturn. Through trial and error you will gain awareness of the best fabrics to use.

## How much fabric should you buy?

Quilters continually struggle with the dilemma of deciding how much fabric to purchase. Whether it is fabric for an individual quilt project or fabric for their personal fabric inventory, quilters often second-guess themselves when it comes to purchasing fabric. If you have selected a pattern, the fabric requirements are typically listed, providing you with a guide for the required fabric amounts. If you're like me, however, you are purchasing fabric as you see it in the quilt shops without a pattern in mind.

When purchasing fabrics for your inventory, you need to consider the key color elements. Look at the fabric's scale, design motif and color combinations. If it's a large-scale fabric intended for outer border strips, purchase at least three yards for that future project. It is better to have too much fabric than not enough.

Appliqué quilters are always looking for new, interesting fabrics. If you find a fabric you can't resist, buy a minimum of a half yard. Keep in mind that in the world of appliqué, you need small amounts of a large variety of appliqué fabrics. A fat quarter will go far when used for small appliqué pieces. Your fabrics are your color palette.

Organize your appliqué fabrics first by color and then by value. Stack them on open shelves so you can see the full collection and have it available when selecting fabrics for a project. Avoid organizing them in closed bins; your appliqué fabrics should be visible and readily available. Large cuts of fabric have a different use and should be stacked separately from your appliqué fabric collection.

# Angela Says

*"Do not stock up on backing fabric. It is better to buy backing fabric with a specific quilt project in mind so it coordinates with the front of the quilt."*

Vintage Venetian features layered appliqués, inside and outside points and curves.

GARDEN
GALLERY

# needleturn appliqué

In this section you will learn everything needed to create beautiful needleturn appliqué projects. Begin with preparing the appliqué shapes and transferring the design and move on to learning the appliqué stitch. Inside and outside points, curves and deep "'V" points are covered. Learn several methods for making circles, stems and vines— shapes that are used in a multitude of appliqué patterns. Finally, try your hand at reverse appliqué, layering shapes and embellishing with embroidery stitches.

# needleturn appliqué preparation

The preparation process for needleturn appliqué is divided into two steps: preparing the appliqué shapes and transferring the design. The most time-consuming task of the preparation is deciding which of the selected fabrics to use and where to place them on the appliqué design. Sometimes it takes the auditioning of many fabrics before being satisfied with the selection. Needleturn appliqué is very portable as long as the preparation of appliqué shapes is completed ahead of time.

### Numbering the shapes and pattern

When starting a new appliqué project, it is important to become familiar with the pattern. Each individual appliqué shape should be numbered in the order it will be appliquéd onto the background fabric.

The order in which the appliqué shapes are numbered is determined by the stitching order. The underlayered appliqué shapes (1 and 3 in example) must be appliquéd before stitching appliqué shapes (2 and 4 in example) on top.

# preparing the appliqué shapes

Templates are needed when tracing the appliqué shapes onto fabric. Template plastic and freezer paper are two of the most popular materials for creating appliqué templates.

## Template Plastic Method

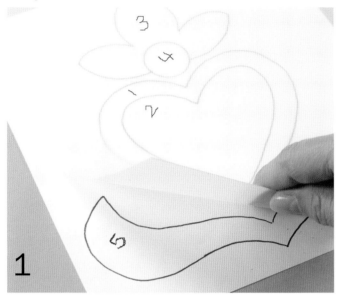

1

2

Template plastic sheets are transparent, so there is no need for a light source when tracing the appliqué shapes. Place the template plastic over the pattern.

Trace the shapes onto the plastic using a template marking pencil or fine-line permanent marker. Using a paper or all-purpose scissors, cut the shapes out directly on the traced lines.

## Freezer Paper Method

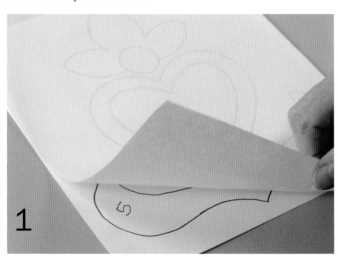

1

2

Freezer paper is wonderful for making templates. It has a waxy side and a dull paper side. Place the freezer paper, waxy side down, over the pattern. Trace the appliqué shapes onto the dull side of the freezer paper using a permanent marking pencil. Label each shape to match the numbers shown on the pattern.

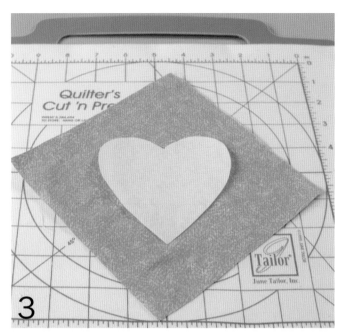

3

After tracing, cut the template out on the traced line. Accuracy is important when tracing and cutting out the templates.

4

Iron the freezer paper templates, waxy side down, to the right side of the applique fabric. Use a hot dry iron for best results.

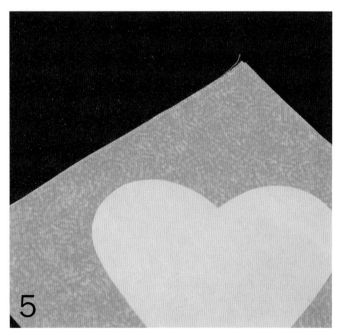

5

Place the appliqué fabric right side up on the sandpaper board. The sandpaper grips the fabric, making the templates easier to trace around.

6

Use a Sewline™ pencil, black for light fabric and white for dark, and trace around the freezer paper. The traced line will be the fold guideline when stitching.

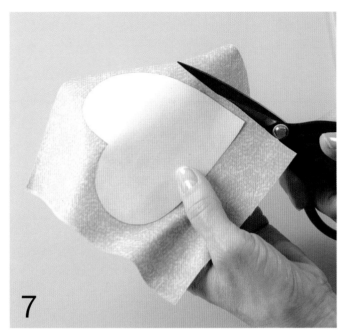

**7**

To create a seam allowance, trim the appliqué shape approximately 3/16" from the edge of the paper template.

## Angela Says

*"If working with a symmetrical design, fold the freezer paper in half and trace only half the design. Staple the layers of freezer paper before cutting out the shapes. Cut through both layers of the folded freezer paper to create a template that is perfectly symmetrical."*

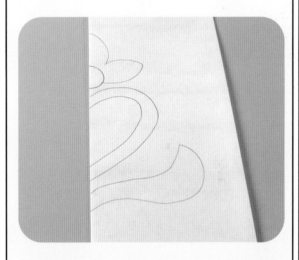

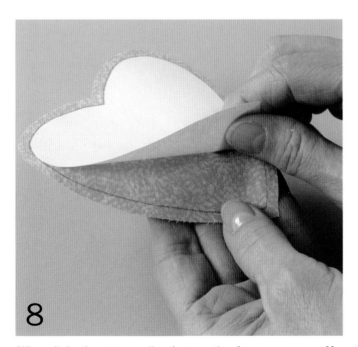

**8**

When it is time to appliqué, tear the freezer paper off the fabric shape and pin the appliqué shape onto the background fabric.

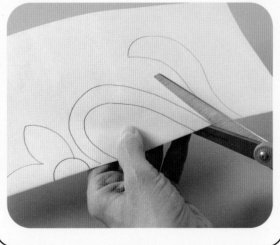

# transferring the design

Cut the applique background fabric at least 1/2" larger on all sides than the finished size of your block. For example, if the finished size of your block is 16-1/2", cut the background fabric 17-1/2" or 18" square. Enlarging the size of the background fabric will compensate for any puckering or raveling that may occur from handling the fabric.

1

2

The chalk pencil tracings are to indicate placement of the appliqué pieces. Use a white or dark gray chalk pencil to trace approximately 1/8" within each pattern shape onto the background fabric. Use only one line when showing stem placement. By tracing within the pattern lines, the chalk markings will be covered by the appliqué pieces.

## Tracing Method

One method of transferring the design is to trace the pattern onto the background fabric. Ideally the pattern is taped over a light box. If a light box is not available, tape the pattern to a sunny window or on a glass table top with a light under it. Use painter's tape to tape the fabric over the pattern. This will eliminate any shifting.

To find the center point on your background fabric, fold the fabric in quarters and finger press the folded point. This is helpful when tracing the pattern onto the background fabric.

### Angela Says

*"The only marking pencil I recommend using when transferring the design to the background fabric is the General's® chalk pencil in white or dark gray. This pencil wears away and can be easily erased. Do not use chalk pencils with color dye as the dye can be difficult to remove from the fabric. In fact, it is nearly impossible."*

## Overlay Method

A transfer method preferred by many quilters is the overlay method. It is preferred because it eliminates any markings on the background fabric.

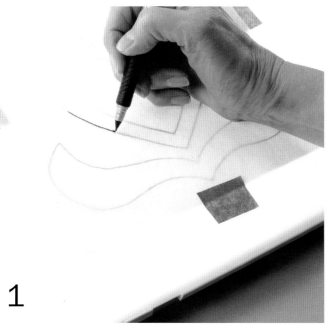

**1**

For this method use a permanent marker and trace the entire design onto a light-weight, nonfusible interfacing such as Pattern Ease.

**2**

After tracing, layer the traced overlay on top of the background fabric. Stitch along the top edge, attaching the two layers.

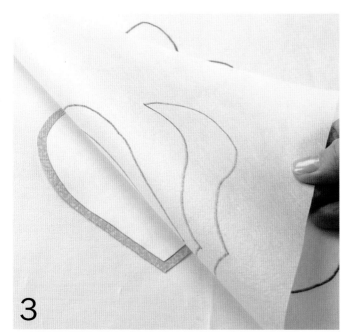

**3**

Slide a prepared appliqué shape in place on the background fabric following the guidelines on the overlay. After positioning the appliqué piece, remove the freezer paper and pin in place. Flip the overlay material out of the way and stitch the appliqué piece in place. Repeat this procedure with each appliqué shape to complete the appliqué design.

# stitching the appliqué

Now that the appliquéd shapes have been prepared, you can begin stitching them in place.

## Threading the Needle

Thread is woven with a definite directional weave, so thread your needle before clipping the thread off the spool. This will help eliminate tangles and knots in your thread while stitching. Clip a 15" to 18" length of thread.

### Angela Says

*"Running thread through Thread Heaven will help eliminate tangles and knots in the thread."*

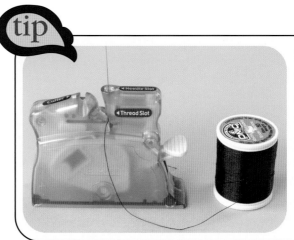

Straw needles are very thin and can be difficult to thread. Use a needle threader to make it easier.

## Tying the Knot

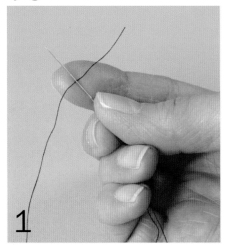

**1** To achieve a perfect knot, hold the end of the thread to the right and place the needle over the thread.

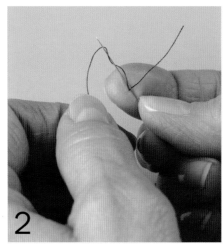

**2** From the left, wrap the thread around the needle two or three times.

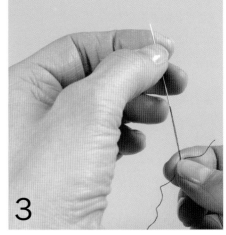

**3** Hold the wrapped thread on the needle and pull the needle up like a rocket ship. A perfect knot is created every time.

### Angela Says

*"Instead of using a thimble to protect my middle finger from a needle puncture, I prefer a latex finger protector called Finger Gloves™. It doesn't feel heavy or bulky while stitching."*

## The Appliqué Stitch

Use 3/4" appliqué pins and pin the shapes to the background fabric from the back to avoid catching the thread on the pins. I prefer the Foxglove Cottage appliqué pins because they are so thin.

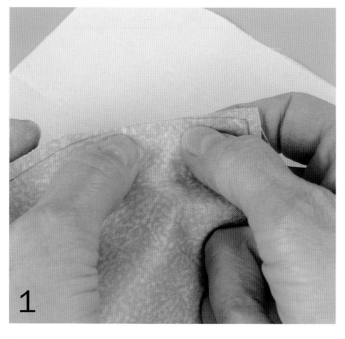

1

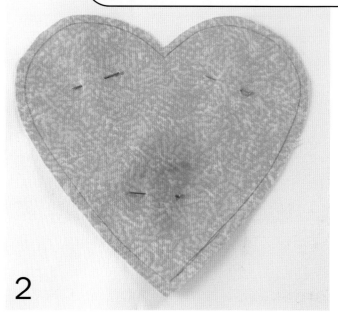

2

Finger-press the seam allowance along the traced line of the appliqué shape. Fabric has a bit of memory, and finger-pressing will help when sweeping the seam allowance under with the needle.

Pin the appliqué shapes to the background fabric.

tip

It is sometimes helpful to baste the shapes onto the background fabric before appliquéing. Larger appliqué shapes have a tendency to shift while being stitched in place.

Whether you hold the needle in the right or left hand, the other hand is also important. The thumb and middle finger hold everything in place, smoothing the turned-under seam allowance so pleating does not occur. When appliquéing, the focus is on the area approximately 1/2" in front of the needle.

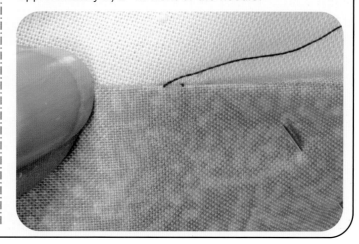

35

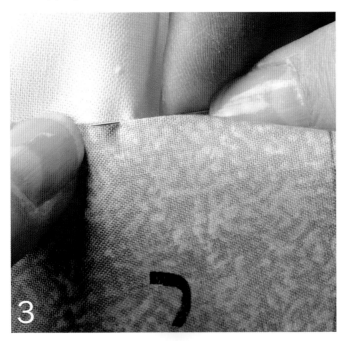

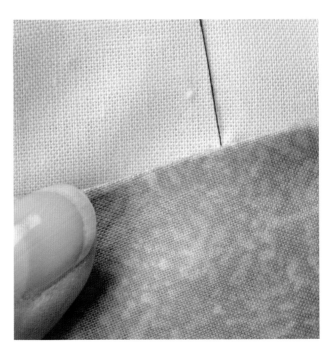

Select a starting point for stitching, preferably on a straight edge of an appliqué shape. If possible, avoid starting on curves and never start on an inside or outside point. Using the straw needle, sweep the seam allowance under on the traced line. Insert the needle into the background fabric and come up, catching the folded edge of the appliqué fabric with the tip of your needle. Make sure the thread knot is tucked behind the appliqué shape.

**NOTE:** *Contrasting thread was used to illustrate the stitching technique. For your project, use a thread that matches the appliqué shapes.*

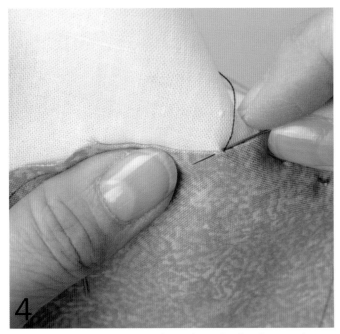

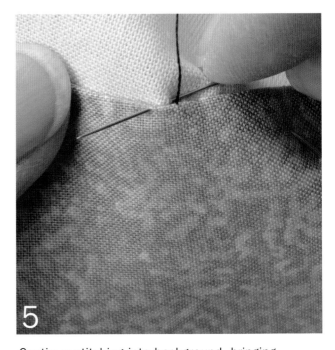

The needle goes directly down into the background fabric next to where it entered the folded edge. This step ensures the least amount of thread will be showing on the right side.

Continue stitching into background, bringing needle tip up, and catching appliqué edge.

**NOTE:** *Small stitches will be visible on the wrong side of background fabric. The stitches should be consistent in size, averaging 8-10 stitches per inch.*

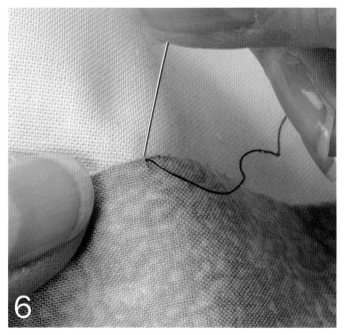

To finish stitching, insert needle down through background fabric and turn appliqué piece over.

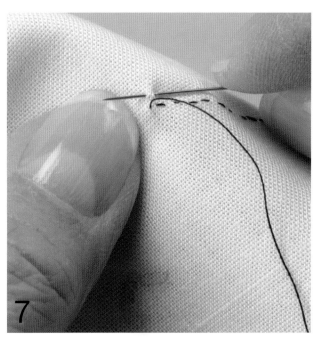

Take two or three back stitches into background fabric.

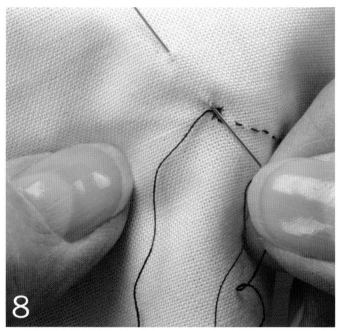

Work the needle between the appliqué piece and background fabric. To finish, snip the thread.

The stitches on the front of the appliqué will not be visible when using a thread color that matches the appliqué.

# stitching points

## Stitching Inside Points

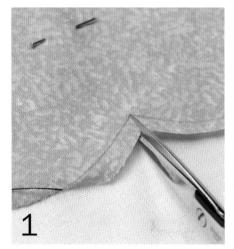

**1**

When approaching an inside point, stop and clip the point to the traced line on the fabric. It is important that the clip is made straight into the point. Do not clip at an angle. This is when a scissors with a very fine point is necessary.

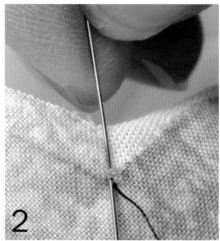

**2**

After clipping, sweep the needle between the appliqué and background fabric to turn under the seam allowance. Stitch along one side of the clipped point. Since clipping the seam allowance weakens the fabric, use very small stitches as you get closer to the clip.

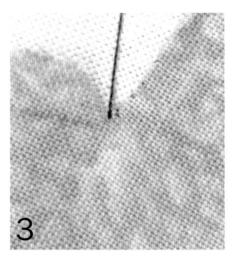

**3**

Take one stitch directly on the clip. Any more than one stitch clutters the clipped area and the extra stitch will show.

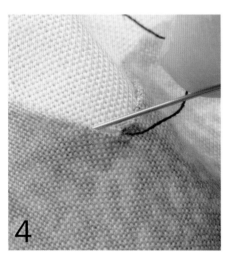

**4**

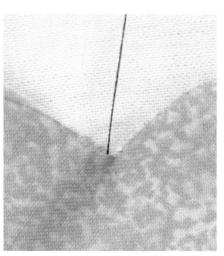

Sweep the seam allowance under on the remaining side of the clip. Continue stitching with very small stitches. The inside point is now complete.

On an inside point, there will be one small stitch before the clip, the stitch on the clip, and a small stitch on the other side of the clip.

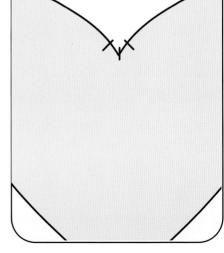

## Stitching Outside Points

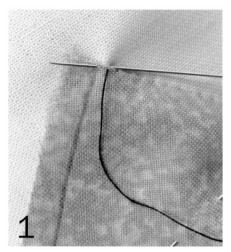

1

Stitching an outside point requires three successive folds of the seam allowance with three stitches. The first fold of the seam allowance is on the right side of the point. Take a stitch along the turned edge.

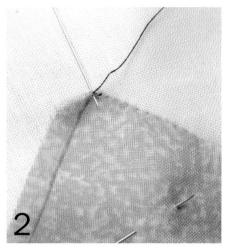

2

The second fold of the seam allowance is folded to allow for a stitch directly on the point.

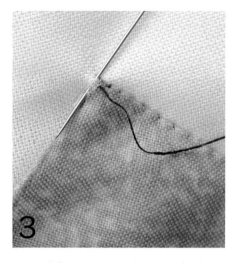

3

After taking the second stitch directly on the point, turn under the seam allowance on the remaining side of the point and take the third stitch. The outside point is now complete.

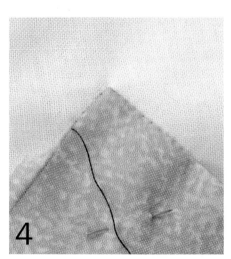

4

Continue sweeping the seam under and stitching as before.

tip

If working with a narrow outside point, the tail of the folded seam allowance may be clipped.

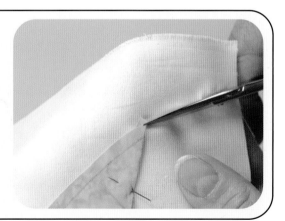

# stitching inside deep "V" points

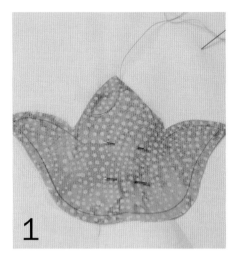

**1**

Deep, narrow "V" points can be difficult to needleturn.

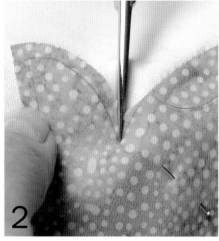

**2**

Clip the inside point.

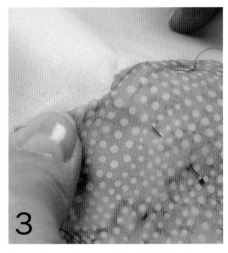

**3**

Turn back the appliqué fabric for easy access to the inner point.

## Angela Says

*"Narrow "V" points are difficult when the fabric begins to ravel or fray at the clip. A batik fabric works well because it requires less seam allowance and usually does not fray."*

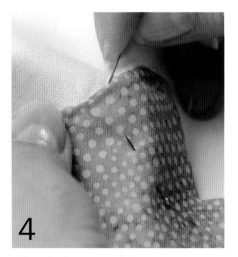

**4**

Stitch to the clip of the point.

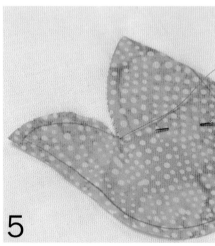

**5**

Stitch directly on the clip. Unfold the appliqué fabric.

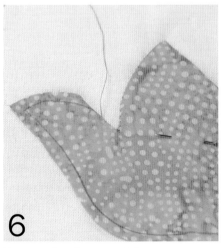

**6**

Turn under the remaining seam allowance to complete the narrow, inside point.

# stitching curves

Outside curves should never be clipped. The fabric will naturally turn on an outside (convex) curve, so clipping is unnecessary.

The only time it is necessary to clip into the seam allowance is when stitching an inside point or when preparing to stitch an inside (concave) curve. Normally you would avoid clipping into the seam allowance because it weakens the fabric; however it cannot be avoided with a concave curve or inside point.

## Outside (Convex) Curves

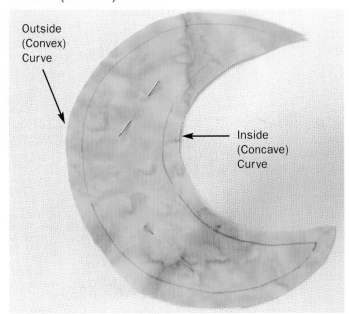

The trick to outside curves is to take smaller stitches and continuously make adjustments as you are turning under the seam allowance. Using small stitches will help eliminate unwanted points that can develop along an outside curve.

## Inside (Concave) Curves

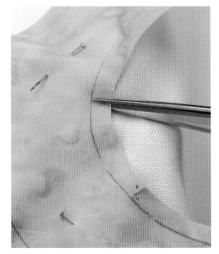

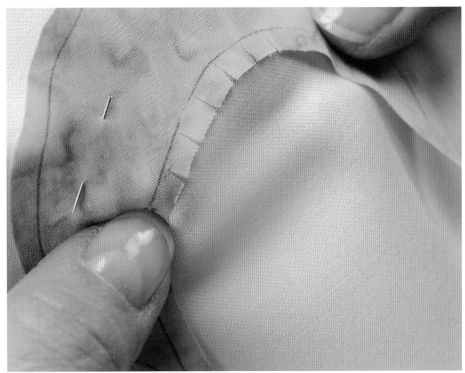

Clip the seam allowance approximately every 1/4" along a concave curve. Make sure to clip to the traced line on the appliqué fabric.
After clipping, begin appliquéing using small stitches to reinforce the clipped edge.

# additional appliqué techniques

Circles, stems and vines are found in many appliqué projects. These shapes are quick and easy to make using the techniques shown.

## Circles

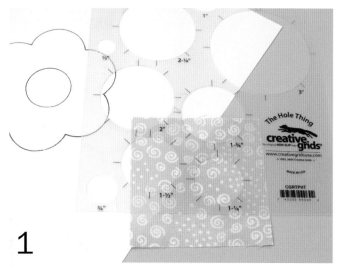

**1**

It is almost impossible to trace a perfect circle, so instead of preparing your own template, purchase a circle template that includes a variety of sizes.

**2**

Select the size you need and use the template to transfer the circle to the appliqué fabric.

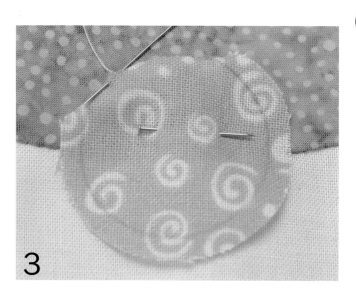

**3**

When needleturning a circle, use an 1/8" seam allowance. Take small stitches and readjust the seam allowance with each stitch.

Collect fabric with fun circle motifs to fussy-cut and incorporate into your designs.

An alternative to needleturning the circles is to make them ahead of time using a product such as Perfect Circles® by Karen Kay Buckley. This product includes a large assortment of Mylar circle shapes.

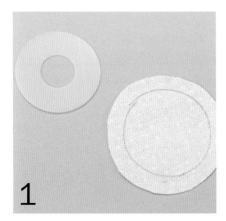

**1**

Trace the Mylar circle template onto the wrong side of the appliqué fabric. Cut around the circle leaving a 1/4" seam allowance.

**2**

Knot the end of a strong thread and baste-stitch in the seam allowance around the circle.

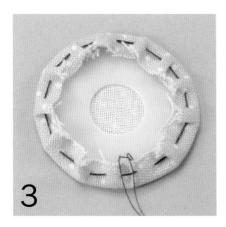

**3**

Place the Mylar template into the circle and gather the basting stitches around the template by gently pulling the thread ends.

**4**

Use Magic Sizing spray starch and a medium-heat, dry iron. Press and mold the fabric around the Mylar circle template. Loosen the basting stitch and remove the Mylar circle. Pull the thread to close the gathered circle. Press and stitch to the fabric surface.

**Shadowing**

Sometimes the turned-under seams create a shadowing effect.

Shadowing occurs when an appliqué fabric is lighter than the background fabric and the turned-under seam allowance shows through the appliqué shape.

To prevent this from happening, a lightweight muslin or interfacing can be inserted underneath the circle before stitching. Use a lightweight batting to give the finished circle added dimension.

## Stems

There are numerous techniques and tools available for creating appliqué stems. Stems are an important feature in many appliqué designs. If the design has curved stems, the stems must be made on the bias. The following stem techniques work well with straight-of-grain or bias fabric strips.

### True Bias

To determine the true bias of a fabric, fold the left edge over to meet the selvage. The diagonal fold is the true bias. Cut off the fabric fold and cut stems or vines from the remaining piece using templates or bias strips.

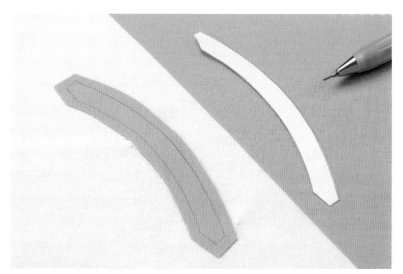

> **tip**
>
> Collect striped fabrics to enhance appliqué stems.
>
> Magic Sizing spray starch and a steam iron can be used when preparing and pressing stems.

### Stem Templates

Appliqué stems can be made by creating a template and tracing around it. If making a short, straight or curved stem, a template works well. If the stem is curved, it will be necessary to clip on the concave curve within the seam allowance. Always stitch the concave side of the stem first.

### Longer Bias Stems

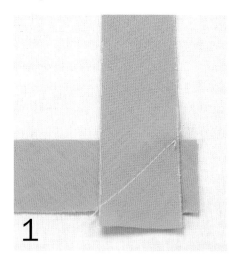

If longer bias stems are needed, lay fabric strips right sides together at a right angle and draw a line corner to corner. Stitch along the drawn line. Trim 1/4" from stitch line.

Press seam open. If using bias press bars, press seams to one side so that the open seams will not catch when the pressing bar is inserted in the fabric sleeve.

## Bias Stems and Vines

The following methods for creating bias stems and vines will ensure a consistent width in your finished pieces. Try each method to see which you prefer.

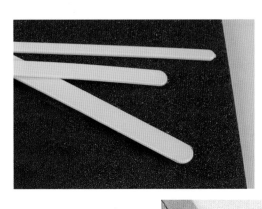

## Bias Press Bars

Bias press bars are a heat-resistant tool designed for creating stems and vines. The bias bars are available in 1/8", 3/16", 1/4", 3/8", and 1/2" sizes.

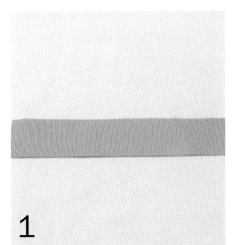

**1**

Cut the fabric strips 1" to 1-1/2" in width. Fold the fabric strips in half lengthwise, right sides together, and press.

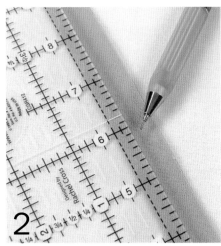

**2**

After determining which size bar to use, measure from the fold line and draw a line slightly larger than the width of the selected bias bar.

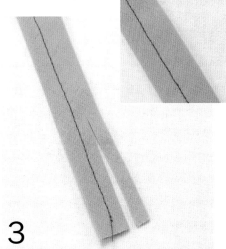

**3**

Stitch along the drawn line to form a sleeve. Trim, leaving slightly less seam allowance than the width of the stem sleeve.

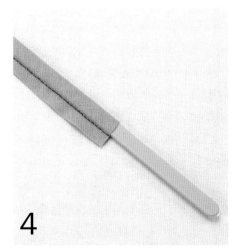

**4**

Insert the bias bar into the opening of the fabric sleeve.

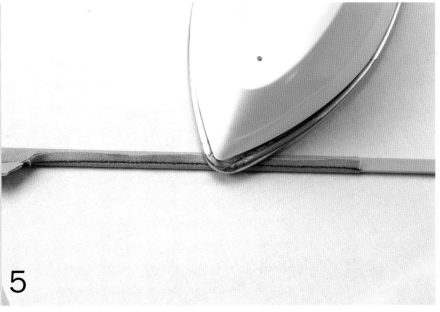

**5**

Roll the seam allowance to the flat side of the bar and steam press. If the fabric sleeve is long, continue sliding the vinyl bar through the fabric sleeve and steam press until completed.

## Bias Tape Maker

The bias tape maker is another tool that ensures consistent widths for stems and vines. It is available in a variety of widths.

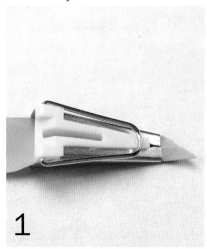

**1**

Trim the end of the fabric strip on an angle. Insert this end through the bias tape maker. Use a stiletto or long straight pin to help work the fabric through the bias tape maker.

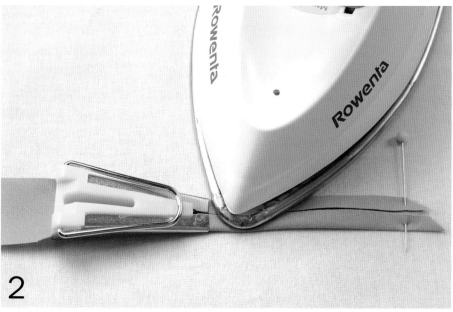

**2**

Pin the end of the fabric strip to the ironing board and push the bias tape maker along with the iron.

## Bias Strips without Bias Bars

With this method, no bias bars are needed. You simply cut fabric strips on the bias in the size you need. Use the formula and examples provided to determine how wide to cut your strips.

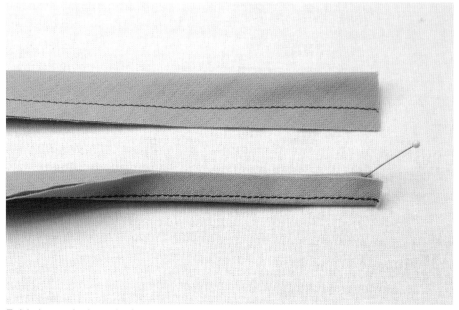

Fold the strip lengthwise, wrong sides together, and machine stitch 1/4" from the raw edge. Fold again and steam press so that the stitching line does not show.

To make bias strips without bars, cut strips three times wider than the desired finished width of the stem or vine. For example, if you want bias strips to finish 1/2", cut strips 1-1/2". Other examples are shown below.

| Desired Finished Size | Cut Strips |
|---|---|
| 1/4" | 3/4" |
| 3/8" | 1-1/8" |
| 1/2" | 1-1/2" |
| 5/8" | 1-7/8" |
| 3/4" | 2-1/4" |
| 1" | 3" |

## Layering Appliqué Shapes

A more complicated appliqué pattern can have several appliqué shapes in one block design. There is no need to panic, the design will be completed by stitching one piece at a time. Layering one appliqué shape on top or next to another is actually easier because the stitching does not go around the entire appliqué shape.

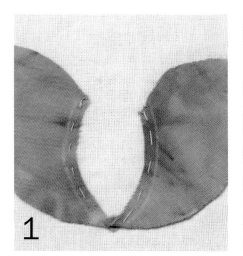

When layering appliqué shapes, do not needleturn the seam allowances that will be overlapped with another appliqué shape. Instead, baste the seam allowance to the background fabric. The next appliqué shape will be lined up on the previous shape and cover the basting stitches.

Place the next appliqué shape on top of the first one, covering the basting stitches. Appliqué in place.

As shown in the example above, multiple appliqué shapes can be layered.

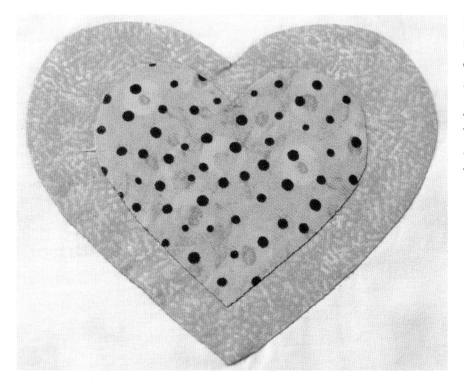

If layering smaller shapes on top of larger ones, make sure the smaller one is centered properly on the larger appliqué shape.

After appliquéing, do not cut away the background fabric under the appliqué shape, as it weakens the background fabric.

## Reverse Appliqué

Reverse appliqué is the process of cutting and stitching within an appliqué shape to expose the fabric underneath. The technique adds to the dimensional quality of the finished appliqué project. Contrasting fabrics are necessary for this technique to be successful.

1

Use freezer paper to make your templates. Trace the outside and inside lines onto the freezer paper. Cut along the inside and outside lines to create the overlay (top) and underlay (bottom) templates.

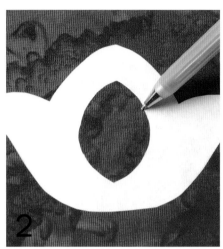

2

Press and trace the inside and outside edges onto the overlay fabric.

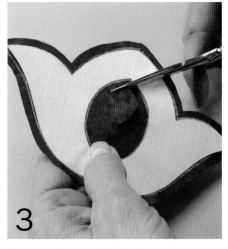

3

Cut out the appliqué shape. Remember to allow for seam allowances along the outside and inside tracing lines. Clip the inside, concave, and curved seam allowances, as well as the inside points. Refer to pages 38 and 41.

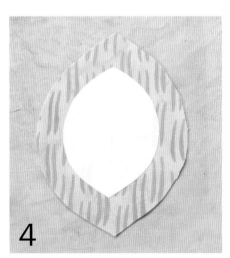

4

Iron the freezer paper to the underlay fabric. Do not trace, but cut the shape as large as possible without extending beyond the outside perimeter of the overlay appliqué shape.

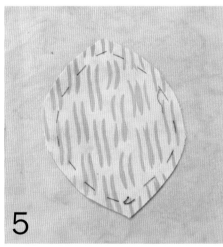

5

Remove the freezer paper template and baste the underlay fabric in place on the background fabric.

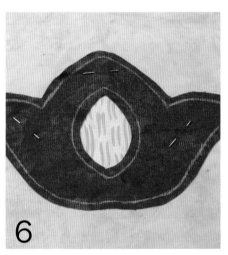

6

Position the overlay appliqué shape over the underlay shape and pin in place.

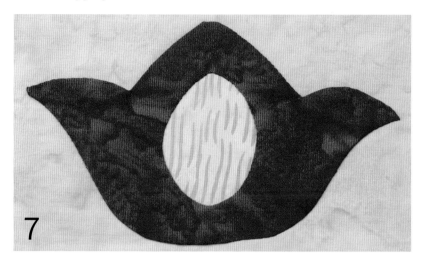

Needleturn the inside edge first, and then proceed to stitch the outside edge to complete the process.

---

## Joining Appliqué Shapes

The technique of joining two appliqué shapes into one is used because it is often easier to stitch two difficult pieces together before appliquéing them to the background fabric. This method eliminates trying to appliqué extremely narrow points.

Looking at the photo of the twisted leaf, it is obvious the very narrow fabric points in this design will be difficult to needleturn. Instead of struggling to appliqué these two fine points, try joining the two appliqué shapes together.

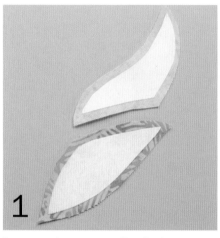

Prepare the two appliqué shapes, referring to page 29.

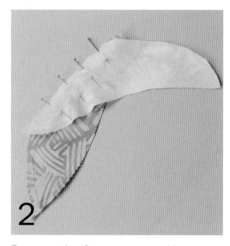

Remove the freezer paper. You may prefer to leave the freezer paper on the fabric to assist in matching lines. Place the appliqué shapes right sides together.

Hand or machine stitch through the two thicknesses. Press seam allowances open.

The two appliqué pieces are now ready to be appliquéd as a whole piece. The two narrow points have been eliminated.

# embellishing the appliqué

To embellish means to enhance or decorate. One of the best ways to embellish appliqué is with embroidery. There is a large variety of embroidery stitches that can be incorporated into appliqué projects. Two of the most common stitches are shown.

## Stem Stitch

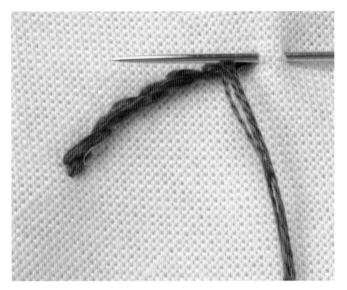

Most of us are familiar with the stem stitch. It is usually taught to children when embroidering on pillowcases and dish towels. A single row of stem stitches can be used in appliqué designs to create a delicate vine, while a double row creates a heavier stem.

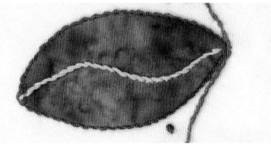

The Stem Stitch can also be used to outline an appliqué shape and give it a finished look. If the appliqué shape is blending into the background fabric, use the stem stitch in a contrasting thread to make the appliqué shape pop.

To create the Stem Stitch, work from left to right and take a small stitch in the fabric. Bring the needle up at the end of the previous stitch. Continue until the design is complete.

## French Knot

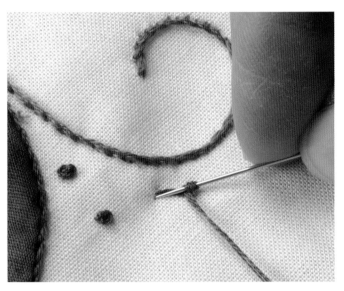

A French Knot is a raised knot that adds an interesting dimensional look to appliqué. It is created by wrapping the thread around an embroidery needle. I often use it in the center of my appliqué flowers.

To make a French Knot, wrap the thread around the needle three to five times. Push the needle back down into the fabric where it came up. Keep the thread wraps close to the fabric. Keep in mind the more times the thread is wrapped around the needle, the larger the knot will be.

## Threads and Needles for Embellishing

A double-mercerized six-strand divisible embroidery thread is perfect when creating embroidery stitches. Divide the six strands and stitch with three at a time. For a more delicate appearance use only two strands. Other great choices for the embroidery are size 8 pearl cotton or size 12 cotton. There are many threads available in a large array of colors, as well as variegated threads. A size 10 embroidery needle works well with these threads.

## Favorites

### Embroidery Needles
- Foxglove Cottage (9, 10, 11)

### Embroidery Thread
- DMC® Floss, Pearl Cotton size 8 and YLI size 12

# finishing techniques

When the appliqué blocks are complete, examine them for pencil or chalk markings. It is important to remove all markings before pressing since the hot temperature of the iron will heat-set any unwanted marks, making them impossible to remove. If chalk or pencil marks need to be removed, place the appliquéd block on the sandpaper board and gently erase any marks.

After removing the markings, the blocks are ready for pressing. Place a thick towel on the ironing surface and lay the appliqué block right side down on it. Gently steam press the block. After pressing, trim the block to the unfinished size according to the pattern. When trimming the appliqué blocks, be sure to measure twice and cut once. Be certain that the appliqué design remains centered when trimming the block.

# projects

Stitch the fun projects on the following pages using the needleturn appliqué techniques you have just learned. Or, be inspired to create your own unique needleturn appliqué masterpiece. Full-size patterns are included to make quick work of transferring the designs.

# Bloomin' Heart

Quilt designed, made and quilted by Angela Lawrence.

# wall hanging

*Finished Size: 13" x 13"*

*This darling miniature wall hanging is a simple design featuring a heart shape.*
*The design reinforces curves, inside and outside points, as well as circles.*

## Fabric Requirements

### Background (Appliqué Block)
1 Fat Quarter

### Border
1/4 yard

### Backing
1 Fat Quarter

### Binding
1/4 yard

### Batting
19" x 19"

## Appliqué Fabric Requirements

### Large Heart
7" x 7" Square

### Small Heart
7" x 7" Square

### Blossom
5" x 5" Square

### Blossom Center
3" x 3" Square

### Leaf
5" x 10" Rectangle

## Cutting Instructions

*Note: wof indicates width of fabric*

From background fabric, cut:
- (1) 11" square for appliqué block.

From border fabric, cut:
- (2) 2-1/4" x wof strips, from these strips cut:
  (2) 2-1/4" x 9-1/2" strips for side borders and
  (2) 2-1/4" x 13" strips for top and bottom borders.

From binding fabric, cut:
- (2) 2-1/4" x wof strips.

From backing fabric, cut:
- 19" square.

## Preparing the Appliquéd Block

1. Refer to pages 26 - 33 to prepare the appliqué shapes and 11" background square.

2. Appliqué the shapes to the background square, referring to pages 34 - 41. After completing the appliqué, trim the block to 9-1/2" square.

## Assembling the Wall Hanging

1. Sew the 2-1/4" x 9-1/2" side border strips to opposite sides of the appliquéd block.

2. Sew the 2-1/4" x 13" top and bottom border strips to the top and bottom of the appliquéd block.

## Finishing the Wall Hanging

1. Layer the wall hanging top, batting and backing.

2. Hand-baste or pin the three layers together.

3. Hand or machine quilt.

4. Sew the binding strips together to make one continuous strip and bind the wall hanging.

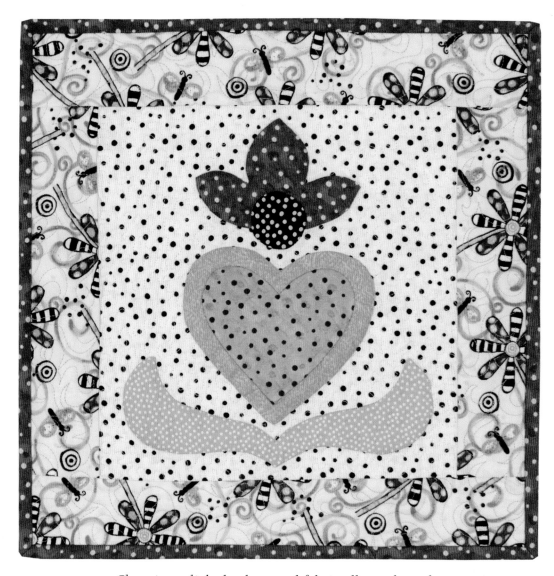

Choosing a light background fabric allows the colors
of the appliqué shapes to stand out.

# Angela's Inspirations

Heart Sampler

# Floral Wreath

Quilt designed, made and quilted by Angela Lawrence.

# wall hanging

*Finished Size: 27-1/2" x 27-1/2"*

*This small quilt is perfect for introducing stems, curves, inside and outside points, as well as circles to your appliqué design.*

## Fabric Requirements

**Background (Appliqué Block)**
1 Fat Quarter

**Inner Border and Binding**
3/8 yard

**Outer Border**
5/8 yard

**Backing**
1 yard

**Batting**
34" square

## Appliqué Fabric Requirements

**Flowers (4)**
12" Square

**Stems**
10" Square

**Leaves**
12" Square

**Flower Centers**
5" Square

## Cutting Instructions

*Note: wof indicates width of fabric*

From background fabric, cut:
• (1) 18" square for appliqué block.

From inner border fabric, cut:
• (2) 1" x wof strips, from these strips cut:
  (2) 1" x 16-1/2" strips for side inner borders and
  (2) 1" x 17-1/2" strips for top and bottom inner borders.

From outer border fabric cut:
• (3) 5-1/2" x wof strips, from these strips cut:
  (2) 5-1/2" x 17-1/2" strips for side outer border and
  (2) 5-1/2" x 27-1/2" strips for top and bottom outer borders.

From binding fabric, cut:
• (4) 2-1/4" x wof strips.

From backing fabric, cut:
• 34" square.

## Preparing the Appliquéd Block

1. Refer to pages 26 - 33 to prepare the appliqué shapes and 18" background square.

2. Appliqué the shapes to the background square, referring to pages 34 - 41. After completing the appliqué, trim the block to 16-1/2" square.

## Assembling the Wall Hanging

1. Sew the 1" x 16-1/2" side inner border strips to opposite sides of the appliquéd block.

2. Sew the 1" x 17-1/2" top and bottom inner border strips to the top and bottom of the appliquéd block.

3. Sew the 5-1/2" x 17-1/2" side outer border strips to opposite sides of the appliquéd block.

4. Sew the 5-1/2" x 27-1/2" top and bottom outer border strips to each side of the appliquéd block.

## Finishing the Wall Hanging

1. Layer the wall hanging top, batting and backing.

2. Hand-baste or pin the three layers together.

3. Hand or machine quilt.

4. Sew the binding strips together to make one continuous strip and bind the wall hanging.

Experiment with striped fabrics when making stems. They are a wonderful addition to the wreath design.

Vivid orange stems accentuate the circular wreath design.

# Angela's Inspirations

Butterfly Boutique

# Tea for Two

Wall Hanging designed,
made and quilted by Angela Lawrence.

# wall hanging

*Finished Size: 21-1/2" x 49-1/2"*

*Appliquéing this lovely wall hanging with its charming teapot, tea cups and saucers will bring back fond childhood memories of porcelain tea sets and tea parties.*

## Fabric Requirements

**Fabric A**
**(appliqué background)**
1/2 yard

**Fabric B**
**(corners, block sashing)**
1/3 yard

**Fabric C (cornerstones)**
1/8 yard

**Fabric D (block border)**
3/8 yard

**Fabric E (sashing)**
1/3 yard

**Fabric F (border)**
1/2 yard

**Binding**
3/8 yard

**Backing**
1-5/8 yards

**Batting**
28" x 55"

## Appliqué Fabric Requirements

**Teapot**
7" Square

**Teapot Trim**
7" Square

**Cups**
12" Square

**Saucers and Handles**
12" Square

**Leaf Motif**
14" Square

## Cutting Instructions

*Note: wof indicates width of fabric*

From Fabric A, cut:
- (1) 15" square.
- (2) 8" squares.

From Fabric B, cut:
- (1) 7" x wof strip, from this strip cut:
  (4) 7" squares.
- (2) 1-1/2" x wof strips, from these strips cut:
  (8) 1-1/2" x 6-1/2" strips.

From Fabric C, cut:
- (8) 1-1/2" squares.

From Fabric D, cut:
- (3) 3" x wof strips, from these strips cut:
  (4) 3" x 8-1/2" strips and
  (4) 3" x 13-1/2" strips.

From Fabric E, cut:
- (4) 1-1/2" x wof strips, from these strips cut:
  (4) 1-1/2" x 13-1/2" strips and
  (2) 1-1/2" x 43-1/2" strips.

*Note: If fabric is not wide enough for the above strip lengths, use the remaining strip to create the lengths required.*

From Fabric F, cut:
- (4) 3-1/2" x wof strips, from these strips cut:
  (2) 3-1/2" x 43-1/2" strips and
  (2) 3-1/2" x 21-1/2" strips.

*Note: If fabric is not wide enough for the above strip lengths, use the remaining strip to create the lengths required.*

From binding fabric, cut:
- (4) 2-1/4" x wof binding strips.

From the backing fabric, cut:
- 28" x 55" rectangle.

## Preparing the Appliquéd Blocks

1. Refer to pages 26 - 33 to prepare the appliqué shapes and background squares.

2. Appliqué the shapes to the corresponding background squares, referring to pages 34 - 41. After completing the appliqué, trim the 15" center block to 13-1/2" square and the 8" top and bottom blocks to 6-1/2" square.

## Assembling the Center Block

1. Use a marking pen or pencil to mark a diagonal line on the wrong side of each Fabric B 7" square.

2. Place a marked 7" square on opposite corners of the 13-1/2" appliquéd center block, right sides together, as shown. Stitch diagonally on the drawn lines through both layers of fabric.

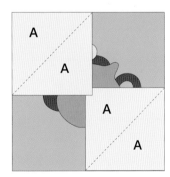

3. Trim 1/4" from the stitched line leaving a 1/4" seam allowance. Fold corners open and press.

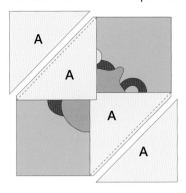

4. Repeat on the other two corners to complete the center block.

If desired, appliqué three leaves on each triangle corner of the center block.

## Assembling the Top and Bottom Blocks

1. Sew a Fabric B 1-1/2" x 6-1/2" strip to each side of the 6-1/2" appliquéd squares.

2. Sew a Fabric C 1-1/2" square to each end of (4) Fabric B 1-1/2" x 6-1/2" strips.

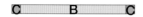

3. Sew the unit made in Step 2 to the top and bottom of the appliquéd square unit as shown.

4. Sew a Fabric D 3" x 8-1/2" strip to each side of the appliquéd block unit.

5. Sew a Fabric D 3" x 13-1/2" strip to the top and bottom of the appliquéd block unit to complete the top and bottom blocks.

*Make 2*

## Assembling the Wall Hanging

1. Lay out the top, bottom and center blocks and (4) Fabric E 1-1/2" x 13-1/2" strips as shown. Sew the pieces together.

2. Sew the Fabric E 1-1/2" x 43-1/2" strips to opposite sides of the piece made in Step 1 to complete the wall hanging center.

3. Sew the Fabric F 3-1/2" x 43-1/2" strips to opposite sides of the wall hanging center.

4. Sew the Fabric F 3-1/2" x 21-1/2" strips to the top and bottom of the wall hanging center.

## Finishing the Wall Hanging

1. Layer the wall hanging top, batting and backing.

2. Hand-baste or pin the three layers together.

3. Hand or machine quilt.

4. Sew the binding strips together to make one continuous strip and bind the wall hanging.

Use a novelty print, such as the border fabric shown, to inspire your design.

The colors in this wall hanging remind me of coffee beans.

# Angela's Inspirations

Totally Teapots

# Simple Delight

Quilt designed and made by Angela Lawrence; quilted by Michele Pettorini.

# wall hanging

*Finished Size: 32½" x 32½"*

*This wall hanging features a large appliqué motif as the centerpiece with a continuous appliquéd vine border. Stem, circle and reverse appliqué techniques are used in this project.*

## Fabric Requirements

**Background (Appliqué Block)**
3/4 yard

**Inner Border**
1/3 yard

**Outer Border**
3/4 yard

**Binding**
1/2 yard

**Backing**
1-1/8 yards

**Batting**
39" Square

## Appliqué Fabric Requirements

**Center Block Vase**
9" Square

**Vase Trim**
9" Square

**Large Leaves**
12" Square

**Small Leaves**
8" Square

**Tulip**
9" Square

**Heart**
4" Square

**Birds**
8" Square

**Small Flowers**
10" Square

**Stems**
1/2 yard

**Miscellaneous shapes**
Variety of fabric scraps

**Borders Bias Vine**
1/2 yard

**Vine Leaves**
12" Square

**Corner Leaves**
12" Square

**Corner Flower Buds**
10" Square

**Flower Center**
6" Square

**Circles**
10" Square

## Cutting Instructions

*Note: wof indicates width of fabric*

From background fabric, cut:
(1) 24-1/2" square for appliqué block.

From inner border fabric, cut:
• (4) 1" x wof strips, from these strips cut:
  (2) 1" x 22-1/2" strips for side inner borders and
  (2) 1" x 23-1/2" strips for top and bottom inner borders.

From outer border fabric, cut:
• (4) 5" x wof strips, from these strips cut:
  (2) 5" x 23-1/2" strips for side outer borders and
  (2) 5" x 32-1/2" strips for top and bottom outer borders.

From binding fabric, cut:
• (5) 2-1/4" x wof strips.

From backing fabric, cut:
• 39" square.

## Preparing the Appliquéd Block and Outer Border Strips

1. Refer to pages 26 - 33 to prepare the appliqué shapes and 24-1/2" background square.

2. Refer to pages 42 - 46 to prepare the circle and bias stem appliqué shapes.

3. Appliqué the shapes to the background square, referring to pages 34 - 41. After completing the appliqué, trim the block to 22-1/2" square.

4. Appliqué the remaining stems, circles and leaves to the outer border strips. Do not appliqué the corner leaves and blossoms to the borders at this time.

## Assembling the Wall Hanging

1. Sew the 1" x 22-1/2" side inner border strips to opposite sides of the appliquéd block.

2. Sew the 1" x 23-1/2" top and bottom inner border strips to the top and bottom of the appliquéd block.

3. Sew the appliquéd side outer border strips to the appliqués block.

4. Sew the appliquéd top and bottom outer border strips to the appliquéd block.

5. Complete the outer border by appliquéing the blossoms and leaves to the corners.

## Finishing the Wall Hanging

1. Layer the wall hanging top, batting and backing.

2. Hand-baste or pin the three layers together.

3. Hand or machine quilt.

4. Sew the binding strips together to make one continuous strip and bind the wall hanging.

# Angela's Inspirations

Folk Art Floral

# Poppies in a Paisley Pot

Quilt designed, made and quilted by Angela Lawrence.

# quilt

*Finished Size: 24-1/2 x 32-1/2*

*I love anything paisley! And, there is nothing more beautiful than a cluster of red poppies in a perennial garden. So what could be better than Poppies in a Paisley Pot?*

## Fabric Requirements

**Fabric A (Appliqué Block and Outer Border)**
7/8 yard

**Inner Border**
1/8 yard

**Outer Border B (Dark)**
1/3 yard

**Cornerstone C**
1/8 yard

**Cornerstone D**
1/4 yard

**Binding**
3/8 yard

**Backing**
1-1/8 yards

**Batting**
31" x 39"

## Appliqué Fabric Requirements

**Large Poppy**
(6) 4" x 6" Rectangles
or (1) 12" Square

**Small Poppies**
(3) 6" Squares
or (1) 12" Square

**Poppy Centers**
6" Square

**Stems**
12" Square

**Paisley Pot**
16" Square

**Paisley Pot Trim**
16" Square

## Cutting Instructions

*Note: wof indicates width of fabric*

From Fabric A, cut:
- (1) 16" x 24" rectangle for appliqué block.
- (10) 4-7/8" squares for outer border.

From inner border fabric, cut:
- (3) 1" x wof strips, from these strips cut:
  (2) 1" x 23-1/2" strips for side inner borders and
  (2) 1" x 16-1/2" strips for top and bottom inner borders.

From outer border fabric B, cut:
- (10) 4-7/8" squares.

From cornerstone fabric C, cut:
- (4) 2-1/2" squares.

From cornerstone fabric D, cut:
- (2) 1-1/2" x wof strips, from these strips cut:
  (8) 1-1/2" x 2-1/2" rectangles and
  (8) 1-1/2" x 4-1/2" rectangles.

From binding fabric, cut:
- (4) 2-1/4" x wof strips.

From backing fabric, cut:
- 31" x 39" rectangle.

## Preparing the Appliquéd Block

1. Refer to pages 26 - 33 to prepare the appliqué shapes and 16" x 24" background rectangle.

2. Appliqué the shapes to the background rectangle, referring to pages 34 - 41. After completing the appliqué work, trim the block to 15-1/2" x 23-1/2".

## Assembling the Pieced Outer Borders

1. Place a 4-7/8" outer border fabric A square on a 4-7/8" outer border fabric B square, right sides together. Draw a diagonal line from corner to corner on the fabric A square.

2. Stitch on either side of the drawn line and through both layers of fabric. Cut on the drawn line and press seams toward the darker fabric to make two half-square triangles. The half-square triangles should measure 4-1/2" square.

3. Repeat Steps 1 and 2 to make (20) half-square triangle blocks.

4. Sew (4) half-square triangle blocks together as shown to make a pieced top border. Repeat to make a pieced bottom border.

*Pieced Top Border*

*Pieced Bottom Border*

5. Sew (6) half-square triangle blocks together as shown to make a pieced side border. Make (2) pieced side borders.

*Make 2*

## Assembling the Border Cornerstones

Sew (2) 1-1/2" x 2-1/2" cornerstone D rectangles to opposite sides of a 2-1/2" x 2-1/2" cornerstone C square. Sew (2) 1-1/2" x 4-1/2" cornerstone D rectangles to the remaining sides of the cornerstone C square to complete a border cornerstone. Make 4 border cornerstones.

## Assembling the Quilt

1. Sew the 1" x 23-1/2" side inner border strips to opposite sides of the appliquéd block.

2. Sew the 1" x 16-1/2" top and bottom inner border strips to the top and bottom of the appliquéd block.

3. Following the diagram for placement, sew the pieced top and bottom borders to the top and bottom of the appliquéd block.

4. Sew (2) border cornerstones to opposite ends of each pieced side border as shown.

5. Following the diagram for placement, sew the pieced side borders to the sides of the appliqué block.

## Finishing the Quilt

1. Layer the quilt top, batting and backing.

2. Hand-baste or pin the three layers together.

3. Hand or machine quilt.

4. Sew the binding strips together to make one continuous strip and bind the quilt.

# Angela's Inspirations

Simply Paisley

# Colonnade

Quilt designed, made and quilted by Angela Lawrence.

# quilt

*Finished Size: 35-1/2" x 51"*

*Create your colonnade quilt by stacking trapezoid shapes and finishing with the simple top and bottom appliqué border.*

## Fabric Requirements

Pieced Trapezoid Blocks
Corners—1/2 yard
Trapezoid Shapes—
Variety of fabrics to
total 1 yard
Vertical Strips
1-1/8 yards
Top and Bottom Border
5/8 yard
Inner Border and Binding
3/4 yard
Backing
1-5/8 yards
Batting
42" x 57"

## Appliqué Fabric Requirements

Tulip
9" Square

Paisley Shapes
and Circles
Variety of fabric scraps

## Cutting Instructions

*Note: wof indicates width of fabric*

From corner fabric, cut:
- (8) 1-3/4" x wof strips, from these strips cut:
  (168) 1-3/4" squares.

From trapezoid fabric, cut:
- (12) 1-3/4" x wof strips, from these strips cut:
  (84) 1-3/4" x 5-1/2" rectangles.

From vertical strips fabric, cut:
- (4) 5-1/2" x 35-1/2" rectangles.

From top and bottom border fabric, cut:
- (1) 9" x 38" rectangle for top border.
- (1) 8" x 38" rectangle for bottom border.

From inner border and binding fabric, cut:
- (4) 1" x wof strips, from these strips cut:
  (4) 1" x 35-1/2" inner border strips.
- (6) 2-1/4" x wof binding strips.

From backing fabric, cut:
- 42" x 57" rectangle.

## Preparing the Appliquéd Borders

1. Refer to pages 26 - 33 to prepare the appliqué shapes and top and bottom border fabric.

2. Appliqué the shapes to the top and bottom borders referring to pages 34 - 41. After completing the appliqué, trim the top border to 8" x 35-1/2" and the bottom border to 6-1/2" x 35-1/2".

## Assembling the Pieced Rectangular Blocks

1. Use a marking pen or pencil to mark a diagonal line on the wrong side of each 1-3/4" square.

2. Place a 1-3/4" square on each end of a 5-1/2" x 1-3/4" rectangle, matching edges and with right sides together. Stitch diagonally on the drawn lines through both layers of fabric.

3. Trim each of the corners leaving a 1/4" seam allowance. Fold corners open and press to make a pieced rectangular block. Make 84 pieced rectangular blocks.

## Assembling the Pieced Columns

Lay out 28 pieced rectangular blocks as shown. Sew the blocks together to make a pieced column. Make 3 pieced columns.

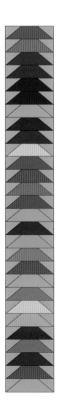

## Assembling the Quilt

1. Lay out four 5-1/2" x 35-1/2" vertical strip rectangles and 3 pieced columns as shown. Sew the pieces together to complete the quilt center.

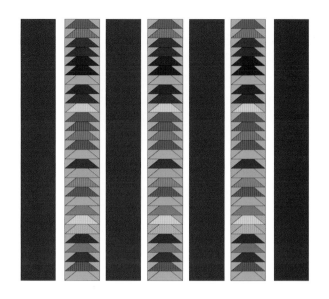

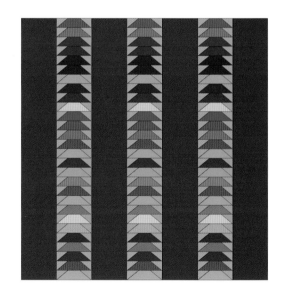

2. Sew a 1" x 35-1/2" inner border strip to the top and bottom edge of the appliquéd borders.

3. Sew the appliquéd borders to the top and bottom of the quilt center.

## Finishing the Quilt

1. Layer the quilt top, batting and backing.

2. Hand-baste or pin the three layers together.

3. Hand or machine quilt. Sew the binding strips together to make one continuous strip and bind the quilt.

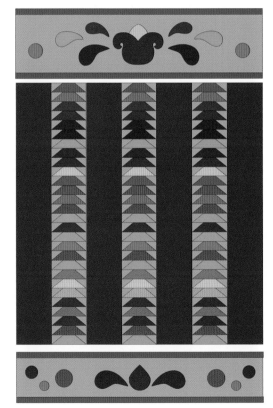

FlutterFly

Quilt designed, made and quilted by Angela Lawrence.

# quilt

*Finished Size: 32" x 32"*

*Where there are flowers, you will find little flying creatures like the FlutterFly. Practice your needleturn appliqué skills while creating these playful blocks.*

## Fabric Requirements

**Background (Appliqué Blocks)**
2/3 yard

**Sashing**
1/4 yard

**Cornerstones**
1/8 yard

**Inner Border**
1/4 yard

**Outer Border**
5/8 yard

**Binding**
1/2 yard

**Backing**
1-1/8 yards

**Batting**
38" Square

## Appliqué Fabric Requirements

**Wings**
(2) 12" Squares

**Bug Bodies**
10" Square

**Antennae Circles**
5" Square

## Cutting Instructions

*Note: wof indicates width of fabric*

From background fabric, cut:
- (4) 11" squares for appliqué blocks.

From sashing fabric, cut:
- (3) 2" x wof strips, from these strips cut:
  (12) 2" x 9-1/2" sashing strips.

From cornerstone fabric, cut:
- (1) 2" x wof strip, from this strip cut:
  (9) 2" squares.

From inner border fabric, cut:
- (4) 1" x wof strips, from these strips cut:
  (2) 1" x 23" side inner border strips and
  (2) 1" x 24" top and bottom inner border strips.

From outer border fabric, cut:
- (4) 4-1/2" x wof strips, from these strips cut:
  (2) 4-1/2" x 24" side outer border strips and
  (2) 4-1/2" x 32" top and bottom outer border strips.

From binding fabric, cut:
- (5) 2-1/4" x wof binding strips.

From backing fabric, cut:
- 38" square.

## Preparing the Appliquéd Blocks

1. Refer to pages 26 - 33 to prepare the appliqué shapes and 11" background squares.

2. Appliqué the shapes to the background squares, referring to pages 34 - 41. After completing the appliqué, use a stem stitch to create the FlutterFly antennae. Refer to page 50.

3. Trim each block to 9-1/2" square.

## Assembling the Quilt

1. Lay out 2 appliqué blocks and (3) 2" x 9-1/2" sashing strips. Sew the pieces together to make a block row. Make 2 block rows.

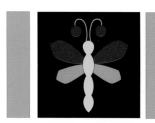 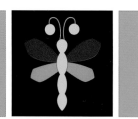

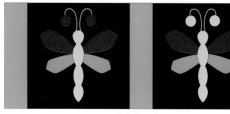

*Make 2*

2. Lay out (3) 2" cornerstone squares and (2) 2" x 9-1/2" sashing strips. Sew the pieces together to make a sashing row. Make 3 sashing rows.

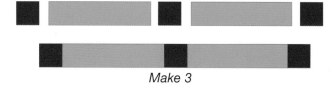

*Make 3*

3. Lay out the 2 block rows and 3 sashing rows. Sew the rows together to make the quilt center.

4. Sew the 1" x 23" side inner border strips to opposite sides of the quilt center. Sew the 1" x 24" top and bottom inner border strips to the top and bottom of the quilt center.

5. Sew the 4-1/2" x 24" side outer border strips to opposite sides of the quilt center.

6. Sew the 4-1/2" x 32" top and bottom outer border strips to the top and bottom of the quilt center.

## Finishing the Quilt

1. Layer the quilt top, batting and backing.

2. Hand-baste or pin the three layers together.

3. Hand or machine quilt.

4. Sew the binding strips together to make one continuous strip and bind the quilt.

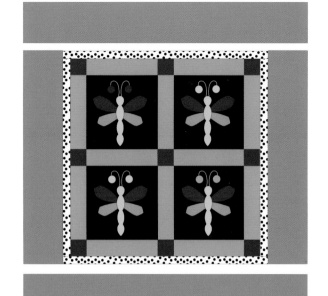

*Angela's Inspirations*

# Fandango

Quilt designed, made and quilted by Angela Lawrence.

# table runner

*Finished Size: 15" x 36"*

*This appliqué pattern uses fabric with circle motif designs. These designs are fussy-cut to enhance the completed appliqué project.*

## Fabric Requirements

**Background (Appliqué Block)**
1/2 yard

**Backing**
5/8 yard

**Binding**
5/8 yard

**Batting**
21" x 42"

## Appliqué Fabric Requirements

**Center Medallion Design**
**(4 fabrics)**
15" Square
12" Square
10" Square
5" Square

**Fan Design**
**(3 fabrics)**
18" Square
15" Square
8" Square

**Bias Vines**
18" Square

**Circles**
**(2 fabrics)**
7" Square
5" Square

## Cutting Instructions

*Note: wof indicates width of fabric*

From background fabric, cut:
• (1) 17" x 43" rectangle for appliqué block.

From binding fabric, cut:
• (3) 2-1/4" x wof strips.
*Note: For bias binding, refer to Binding the Curved Edge on page 86.*

From backing fabric, cut:
• 21" x 42" rectangle.

## Preparing the Appliquéd Block

1. Refer to pages 26 - 33 to prepare the appliqué shapes and background rectangle.

2. Refer to pages 42 - 46 to prepare the circle and bias stem appliqué shapes.

3. Appliqué the shapes to the background rectangle, referring to pages 34 - 41. Embellish the appliqué shapes using the stem stitch if desired. Refer to page 50.

4. After completing the appliqué, trim the rectangle by placing the pattern on top of it and cutting along the edges.
*Note: The pattern includes the binding seam allowance.*

## Binding the Curved Edge

1. Fandango features slightly curved edges, which can be completed using either straight-of-grain or bias binding. A bias binding would be more effective since a more flexible fabric strip will ease nicely around the curves of the table runner.

2. To make a bias binding, you must first find the bias on a square of the fabric. Fold a square of fabric diagonally, matching opposite corners. The bias is the folded diagonal line. Cut 2-1/4" strips at the diagonal fold. An alternative method for finding the bias on a square of fabric is to use a ruler and align the edge of the fabric with the 45-degree line on the ruler.

3. After cutting the bias strips sew them together to make one continuous strip. Fold the continuous strip in half lengthwise, wrong sides together, and press.

## Finishing the Table Runner

1. Layer the table runner, batting and backing.

2. Hand-baste or pin the three layers together.

3. Hand or machine quilt.

4. Sew the bias binding to the table runner top using the same method as for straight-of-grain binding.

A striped background fabric adds an additional design element to the runner.

# Vintage Venetian

Quilt designed and made by Angela Lawrence; quilted by Debbi Treusch.

# quilt

*Finished Size: 45-1/2" x 45-1/2"*

*The traditional snowball block imitates a classic venetian mosaic tile pattern that surrounds an original appliquéd block design.*

## Fabric Requirements

**Background (Appliqué Block)**
5/8 yard

**Snowball Blocks**
Block Centers—
1/8 yard each of 12 fabrics
Corners—3/4 yard

**Borders**
5/8 yard

**Binding**
1/2 yard

**Backing**
3 yards

**Batting**
52" Square

## Appliqué Fabric Requirements

**Large Heart**
12" Square

**Inner Heart**
10" Square

**Heart Petals**
Variety of fabric scraps

**Teardrops**
Variety of fabric scraps

**Center Design**
Variety of fabric scraps

## Cutting Instructions

*Note: wof indicates width of fabric*

From background fabric, cut:

- (1) 20" square for appliqué block.

From snowball block center fabric, cut:

- (12) 4" x wof strips, from these strips cut:
  (108) 4" squares for block centers.

From snowball block corner fabric, cut:

- (17) 1-1/2" x wof strips, from these strips cut:
  (432) 1-1/2" squares for corners.

From border fabric, cut:

- (4) 2" x wof strips, from these strips cut:
  (2) 2" x 18-1/2" top and bottom inner border strips and
  (2) 2" x 21-1/2" side inner border strips.
- (5) 2" x wof strips, from these strips cut:
  (2) 2" x 42-1/2" top and bottom outer border strips and
  (2) 2" x 45-1/2" side outer border strips.

*Note: If fabric is not wide enough for the above strip lengths, use the remaining strip to create the lengths required.*

From binding fabric, cut

- (6) 2-1/4" x wof strips.

From backing fabric, cut:

- (2) 54" lengths.

## Preparing the Appliquéd Block

1. Refer to pages 26 - 33 to prepare the appliqué shapes and background square.

2. Appliqué the shapes to the background square, referring to pages 34 - 41. After completing the appliqué work, trim the block to 18-1/2" square.

## Assembling the Snowball Blocks

1. Use a marking pen or pencil to mark a diagonal line on the wrong side of each 1-1/2" square.

2. Place a 1-1/2" square on each corner of a 4" square, matching edges and with right sides together. Stitch diagonally on the drawn lines through both layers of fabric.

3. Trim each of corners leaving a 1/4" seam allowance. Fold corners open and press to make a snowball block. Make 108 snowball blocks.

*Make 108*

## Assembling the Borders

1. Lay out 3 rows of snowball blocks with 6 blocks in each row as shown. Sew the blocks together in rows and then sew the rows together to make a top snowball border. Repeat to make a bottom snowball border.

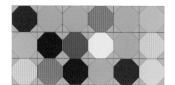

*Make 2*

2. Lay out 3 rows of snowball blocks with 12 blocks in each row as shown. Sew the blocks together in rows and then sew the rows together to make a side snowball border. Make 2 side snowball borders.

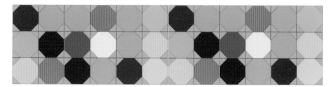

*Make 2*

## Assembling the Quilt

1. Sew the 2" x 18-1/2" top and bottom inner border strips to the top and bottom of the appliquéd block.

2. Sew the 2" x 21-1/2" side inner border strips to the sides of the appliquéd block.

3. Sew the top and bottom snowball borders to the appliquéd block.

4. Sew the side snowball borders to the appliquéd block to complete the quilt center.

5. Sew the 2" x 42-1/2" top and bottom outer border strips to the quilt center.

6. Sew the 2" x 45-1/2" side outer border strips to the quilt center.

## Finishing the Quilt

1. Layer the quilt top, batting and backing.

2. Hand-baste or pin the three layers together.

3. Hand or machine quilt.

4. Sew the binding strips together to make one continuous strip and bind the quilt.

Vintage Venetian takes on a very rich look in dark-toned fabrics.

# General Finishing Instructions

## Backing

Prepare the backing fabric after the quilt top has been completed. The backing fabric should extend past each side of the quilt top by two to three inches. Typically, the crosswise width of fabric is approximately 42" after removing the selvage from the fabric edges. If the quilt top exceeds this width, you will need to piece your back. When piecing the backing fabric, sew the fabric lengths together with 1/2-inch seam allowance and press the seams open.

## Batting

The batting should be the same size as the backing fabric. There are many types and lofts of batting available, but I prefer a low-loft thickness. One of my favorites is an 80 percent cotton/20 percent polyester batting. If you plan to hand quilt, I recommend using a polyester batting. It is easier to work with when taking the needle through the three layers.

## Layering

To prepare for quilting, you must layer the backing, batting and quilt top. Place the backing fabric, right side down, on a flat surface. Use masking or painter's tape to tape the backing fabric to the flat surface, keeping it taut. Lay the batting over the backing fabric. Smooth the batting out evenly over the backing fabric. If you wish, you may tape the batting in place. Lay the quilt top on the batting. Use safety pins or hand-baste the three layers together.

## Quilting

Now that the quilt is layered, it is ready to hand or machine quilt. Regardless of your choice of quilting, it is necessary to first stitch around all the appliqué shapes. I prefer using a very close stitch that is right next to the appliqué shape. The use of small, close stitches provides a raised, dimensional quality to the appliqué on your finished project.

# Binding

1. Once the quilting is complete, trim the layers so the edges are even and the corners are squared.

2. Cut binding strips 2-1/4" x width of fabric. Sew the strips together using a diagonal seam. Trim the seams 1/4" from the sewn line and press open to make one continuous strip.

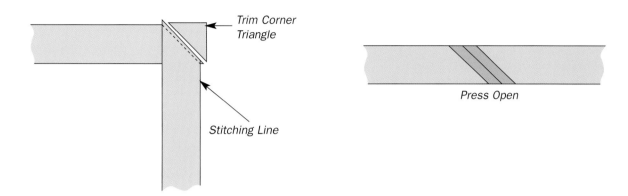

3. Fold the strip in half lengthwise, wrong sides together, and press. Use the strip to bind and complete the quilt.

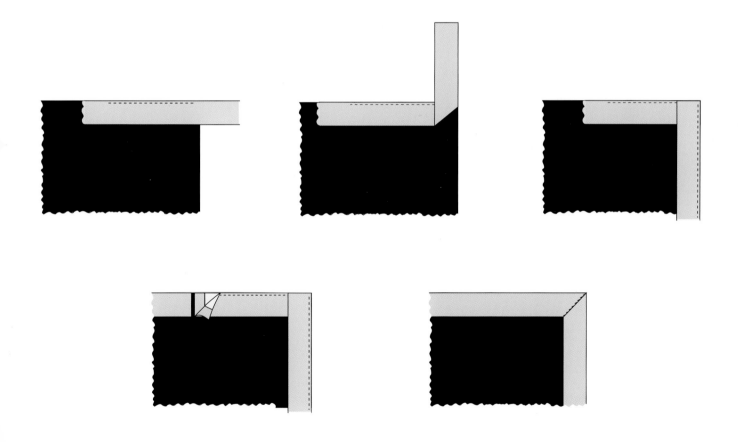

# Resources

## Needles and Threads

**Jeana Kimball Fox Cottage Straw Needles:**
www.jeanakimballquilter.com

**YLI Silk Thread:** www.ylicorp.com

**Kimono™ Silk Thread:** www.superiorthreads.com

**DMC® Cotton Thread:** www.dmc-usa.com

**Mettler Metrosene Thread:** www.amann-mettler.com

**Aurifil™ Mako Cotton Thread:** www.aurifil.com

**Sulky® Cotton Thread:** www.sulky.com

## Scissors

**Karen Kay Buckley Scissors:**
www.karenkaybuckley.com

**Gingher Scissors:** www.gingher.com

## Appliqué Pins

**Fox Cottage Appliqué Pins:**
www.jeanakimballquilter.com

**Clover Appliqué Pins:** www.clover-usa.com

## Marking Tools

**Dritz® Tracing Pencils:** www.dritz.com

**General's® Pastel Chalk Pencils:**
www.generalpencil.com

**Sewline™ Tracing Pencils:** www.sewline-product.com

## Light Sources

**Ott-Lite®:** www.ottlite.com

**Light Box:** www.artograph.com

## Special Tools

**Clover Bias Tape Maker:** www.clover-usa.com

**Clover Bias Press Bar:** www.clover-usa.com

**Creative Grids® Circle Templates:**
www.creativegrids.com

**Perfect Circles® by Karen Kay Buckley:**
www.karenkaybuckley.com

**Sewline™ Fabric Eraser:** www.sewline-product.com

**Bohin Fabric Eraser:** www.bohin.fr/en

**Foxglove Cottage Embroidery Needles:**
www.jeanakimballquilter.com

**DMC® Embroidery Floss:** www.dmc-usa.com

**Weeks Dye Works™ Embroidery Floss:**
www.weeksdyeworks.com

**Finger Gloves™:** www.fingergloves.com

**Thread Heaven:** www.threadheaven.com

**Sewline™ Needle Threader:** www.sewline-product.com

**Clover Needle Threader:** www.clover-usa.com

## Machine Quilters

**Debbi Treusch:** brookrunquiltworks@mchsi.com

**Michele Pettorini:** www.michelescustomquilting.com

**Theresa Porter:** www.etsy.com/shop/meanderingthread

**Landauer Publishing:** www.landauercorp.com

*For more needleturn appliqué patterns and inspiration visit Angela's website, Appliqué After Hours at www.appliquéafterhours.com*

# Acknowledgments

*Making this book a reality comes with much gratitude
and a special "Thank You" to the following:*

*My husband, Bill,* for his encouragement in all my quilting endeavors, this book would not have been written without his love and support.

*My children,* who heard for years that mom was going to write a book!

*Patty Barrett,* for reading my manuscript and giving me confidence as well as professional advice.

*My co-workers* at Creekside Quilting, for their endless support and encouragement.

*Appliqué students,* past and present, who have enriched and inspired my quilt world.

*Landauer Publishing* for sharing their talents and giving me the opportunity to write this book.

*Thank you to Mary Shotwell for allowing us to photograph her Crazy Quilt on page 20
and to Emily Nelson for the use of her personal photography on page 21.
Supplies were provided by Creekside Quilting in Urbandale, Iowa (www.creekside-quilting.com).*

## About the Author

Angela has been teaching needleturn appliqué since 1998. With a degree in education, it was only natural that her love of teaching and passion for quilting would draw her back to the classroom to teach beginning through advanced appliqué workshops.

Angela and her husband, Bill, have six children and two grandchildren and reside in Urbandale, Iowa. Although she enjoys all aspects of quilting, her passion is needleturn appliqué.